AMEN *and* GOOD NIGHT, GOD

School of Divinity

Gardner-Webb University
School of Divinity

This book donated
by

DR. JOHN ROBERTS

A M E N

and

GOOD NIGHT

G O D

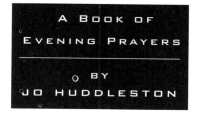

A BOOK OF
EVENING PRAYERS

○ BY
JO HUDDLESTON

Tyndale House Publishers, Inc.
Wheaton, Illinois

Scripture quotations are taken from the *Holy Bible,* New International Version®.
Copyright © 1973, 1978, 1984 by International Bible Society. Used by
permission of Zondervan Publishing House. All rights reserved. The "NIV" and
"New International Version" trademarks are registered in the United States
Patent and Trademark Office by International Bible Society. Use of either
trademark requires permission of International Bible Society.

Library of Congress Cataloging-in-Publication Data

Huddleston, Jo, date
    Amen and good night, God : a book of evening prayers / by Jo Huddleston.
      p. cm.
    ISBN 0-8423-1668-X (pbk.)
    1. Prayers. 2. Christian life. I. Title.
  BV245.H77 1995
  242'.8—dc20   95-33103

Printed in the United States of America

01 00 99 98 97 96 95
7   6   5   4   3   2   1

Do not be anxious about anything, but in everything, by prayer and petition, with thanksgiving, present your requests to God. And the peace of God, which transcends all understanding, will guard your hearts and your minds in Christ Jesus. Philippians 4:6-7

CONTENTS

INTRODUCTION

Some nights while searching for sleep, I realize I blew it again somehow during the day. On other evenings, doubts and misunderstandings flood my memories. Many times as I review and try to release the day, I struggle with hurt feelings and heavy loads. In the still darkness of bedtime, I share these emotions with God in casual, intimate conversation. I may rant and rave, plead, offer gratitude, or even question. God listens because he loves me when it seems nobody else does. Then, when I've allowed God to lift me from my floundering, his healing peace settles me into sleep. God awaits our daily communication. We can bring him our frustrations, and he will replace them with his cleansing and consolation. As you read these pages, may they help you know at day's end that

> *The Lord is faithful to all his promises*
> *and loving toward all he has made.*
> *The Lord upholds all those who fall*
> *and lifts up all who are bowed down.* (Psalm 145:13-14)

ANXIETY

God,

I did a lot of hand-wringing today, working myself into a frenzy of jangled nerves. I anticipated the worst that could happen. Later, I realized everything had gone well, disproving my fearful concerns. You never promised life would always stay anchored, would never break loose in a storm to bob violently on rough seas. Thank you for being my lifeboat in the storms. I should have stopped all my fretting early on and trusted you for safe harbor. You knew all about today. You know all about tomorrow. Please help me to put my every day in your hands.

AMEN *and* GOOD NIGHT, GOD

ANXIETY

God,

How thankful I am that you have promised to care for me if I will allow you to deal with my anxieties! That sounds so simple. But today my old human nature just wouldn't let go. I remained uneasy about this and that, trying to prepare for what might happen. Trying to control the outcome. I guess I must have been afraid of failing, though, because all the time I was organizing and arranging, I braced myself for disappointment. Please help me, Lord, to trust you to remove these fears, supporting me and calming my frustrations.

AMEN *and* GOOD NIGHT, GOD

ANXIETY

God,

I had this bad feeling all day—like impending doom was lurking around every corner. Waiting, ready to snatch at me, defeating my every effort. Instead of being a positive force for you today, Lord, I wasted the day trying to second-guess my next moment, my next hour. I tuned in to the world's principles, not listening to you. Please blow away anxiety's dark cloud, which I've allowed to overstay its visit. Thank you for caring for me in all ways, just as you provide for little birds and the wildflowers in the field.

AMEN *and* GOOD NIGHT, GOD

ASSURANCE

God,

It was touch and go here at the hospital today before the fever finally broke. But my child is out of danger now and improving—thank you, God! Many have marveled at my calm during the worst hours. Because you are my strength and help, I didn't panic. Thank you for staying with me throughout the day. Thank you for calm assurance in all my crisis situations.

AMEN *and* GOOD NIGHT, GOD

ASSURANCE

God,

I need your peaceful assurance to secure me against the whirlwinds of this confusing world. Today I was pushed in one direction and then in another, and the distance between us grew and grew. Like an earthquake had opened up the ground, and you and I stood on opposite edges of the yawning gap. The world tries to pull us apart every day, Lord, hoping I can't cross the wedge it hammers between us. Thank you for your faithfulness in not leaving me helpless — not leaving me alone but rescuing me and calming all my uncertainties.

AMEN *and* GOOD NIGHT, GOD

ASSURANCE

God,

I slipped up too many times today ever to depend on just myself anymore. When I ventured out on my own, not bringing you with me, I faltered and lost my way. But when I finally looked for you, I found you waiting for an invitation to be a part of my life. You're my security blanket. You've promised you'll work everything out if I'll love and obey you. You've given me absolute assurance that, no matter what happens, you will get me through it. Thank you, Lord, for offering me such undeserved grace and mercy.

AMEN *and* GOOD NIGHT, GOD

ATTITUDE

God,

Thank you for giving me joy. Because I trust in you, joy is always with me—like the air in my lungs. When that baseball crashed through my new picture window today, my joy almost surrendered to anger. But, instead, your encouragement settled over me. You helped me operate from a base of joy even in facing this discouragement. I may get irritated or frustrated again tomorrow, but your joy will be there, giving me a needed boost when nothing else can.

A M E N *and* G O O D N I G H T , G O D

ATTITUDE

God,

I think I hurt someone today. Oh, I didn't actually cause physical pain or even insult anybody. Simply because I was in a bad mood, I may have affected someone's day; I may have taken away some of their happiness. Cleanse my heart, God, for it's the wellspring of life. Thank you for helping me start tomorrow with a positive attitude so I won't hurt anyone.

ATTITUDE

God,

I hope you don't mind that I don't go to my knees every time I talk to you. If I did, I'd be kneeling almost all day long. Today I came close to praying continually. I prayed about every little glitch. Thank you for untangling all my confusion today. I praise you for being close, as if you knew I'd need you every time I turned around. Of course you knew, didn't you? I'm so thankful I can approach each day, secure in a prayerful attitude—when I'm asking and when I'm complaining. Also when I'm praising you and when I'm in awe of your majesty. Lord, I'm glad you're at home in my mind as well as in my heart.

AMEN *and* GOOD NIGHT, GOD

BITTERNESS

God,

When I first heard about their unjust words I was shocked. Then I hurt. Deeply. As soon as I was alone, I cried. A lot. They shouldn't have said those things about me. I'm doing the best I can do. As I continued to think about the whole episode, I began to brood. Soon I felt resentment, which quickly grew into grudges against them all. But my grudges won't change what happened this morning. My bitter feelings affect *me* most of all. God, with your love please help my bitterness melt into forgiveness. Let your peace rule in my heart. Thank you for helping me erase today's bad memories.

AMEN *and* GOOD NIGHT, GOD

BITTERNESS

God,

As this evening wore on, my nervous tension increased. I just couldn't go to bed without settling my mind. So I telephoned, even at such a late hour. When she heard my voice, I almost needed a sweater to ward off the chill coming through the phone. But I'm so glad I called. Before hanging up, we both admitted feeling freed from growing resentment over our argument this morning. Lord, thank you that your peace now blooms between my friend and me. I needed your courage to weed out the bitterness that was quickly taking root in my life. Please help me to react as you would, avoiding such confrontations tomorrow.

AMEN *and* GOOD NIGHT, GOD

BOREDOM

God,

I thought I was doing my own thinking, but now I realize I was listening to Satan. The lure of the lifestyle I left behind beckoned through my boredom with a sweet, clear voice. Boredom must be one of Satan's most powerful and subtle weapons. He made my old ways look as attractive as ever. And so inviting. It would have been easy today for me to have stepped across seduction's thin line and into the arms of worldly pleasure. Thank you, Lord, for taking my hand when I reached for guidance out of the slimy waters I'd willingly waded into. Please stay near, helping me defend against all of Satan's weapons.

AMEN *and* GOOD NIGHT, GOD

BURDENS

God,

Thank you for helping me carry my heavy load today. I couldn't have accomplished anything without your strength. I was foolish for acting like the expert, trying to solve all my problems alone. But I can't solve any of them without your help. Thank you for letting me share my burdens with you. When you shouldered my responsibilities today, relief washed over me like sunshine bursting through on a cloudy day. You never fail me. I can sleep well tonight, knowing I've turned everything over to you.

AMEN *and* GOOD NIGHT, GOD

BURDENS

God,

What would I do without you? However weak I am, your strength picks me up. Every day you carry me and my problems. Even when my load is self-made and trivial—as it was today, Lord—you never question. You just let me continue to lay all my troubles on you. Thank you for sharing my emotions and feeling my pain. I can approach tomorrow with shoulders thrown back, ready for whatever the world has in store. Thank you for your support.

AMEN *and* GOOD NIGHT, GOD

BURDENS

God,

I learned a long time ago that I can't do anything without your help. But lessons learned are sometimes soon forgotten. So, here I am, seemingly back at square one with you. But only because the stench of defeat surrounded me today. Almost too late, I realized that I wasn't making any progress alone. In fact, I'd almost surrendered all hope when your promises flashed before me like lightning, bringing me back to reality: the reality that you will not abandon me, Lord. Help me to remember that you don't move away from me; I'm the one who does the moving. Thank you for your loyalty and eagerness to share anything that bothers me.

AMEN *and* GOOD NIGHT, GOD

CHRISTLIKE LIVING

God,

I went to dinner this evening with some new acquaintances and got carried away with their lifestyle. Please forgive me. And the next time I'm invited to go out, please give me the courage to take you with me or not to go at all. Tomorrow I'll try harder to make my life pleasing to you. I promise next time I'll show others I'm honored to have you in my life. Thank you for giving me another try to be like you.

CHRISTLIKE LIVING

God,

No one would ever have guessed whose side I was on this morning. I feel bad that I didn't stand up for what you teach. It's hard to speak out when I'm a minority of one. So I just kept quiet. Please forgive me for hanging back, not helping your cause at all. I should be your feet and your voice, and I wasn't either one today. Thank you for understanding when I'm timid. Please continue to shape me—improvement is bound to come! Thank you for still loving me even though I'm not yet all that you want me to be. This maturing into your likeness may take my whole lifetime!

AMEN *and* GOOD NIGHT, GOD

CHRISTLIKE LIVING

God,

Please help me to be more like you. As I look back over today, I'm convinced I could have achieved more if I'd had more of your qualities, more of your internal graces. Tomorrow I'll try blending some of your personality into mine. I'll include a big helping of patience and an equal amount of kindness. Some self-control and contentment wouldn't hurt, either. Tomorrow I'll offer others your gentleness and humility. Your peace and your love. Lord, help me to display your nature in all my activities and encounters tomorrow. Thank you for showing me your character as my model and my motivation.

AMEN *and* GOOD NIGHT, GOD

COMMITMENT

God,

I tried to accomplish too much today and didn't do my best with anything. I thought I could get around to everything I'd planned, but my energy lagged before the day's end was in sight. God, please help me to realize I can only do so much if I'm to do anything well. And I always want to put you first. May I never give less than 100 percent in my praise and worship of you. Thank you for allowing me to try again!

AMEN *and* GOOD NIGHT, GOD

COMMITMENT

God,

Today did you doubt the wisdom of giving me life when I refused you even a small amount of my time? I'm so stingy, Lord. When I have some free time, I want it for myself. Help me to remember that you give me all my days. Thank you, Lord, for your unselfishness toward me. Help me to give back to you with equal generosity.

COMPLAINING

God,

At every turn today I ran into a brick wall. All my plans fell through, one by one. Again and again I had to back up, rethink, and start from another angle. I complained about the many detours, searching for ways around them. I wouldn't have been so grumpy all day if I had turned to you for workable directions. Thank you that your plans overshadow any threatening roadblocks I may encounter.

COMPLAINING

God,

I'm so thankful you help me to cope with the complaining attitudes around me. When my mate worried today that our child might not pass her test, I answered, "But she may." When pessimists bemoaned our government with their gloom and doom, I pointed out some good things about our country. Jesus didn't go around dragging folks down by spreading bad news. Lord, please help me to continue to look for the brighter side. There always is one if I'll search long enough.

COMPLAINING

God,

I'm just sick and tired of all the griping. Nothing I do ever pleases them. All day long whenever I got one child satisfied, the other one began to whine. When I'd go to pacify that one, then the first child had grown discontent and began grumbling. It's like this all day long, Lord! Almost every day! Why can't they be satisfied when I take care of all their needs and occasionally give them extras? Oh my, listen to me. Does this sound familiar to you? Did I just describe myself? Do I really bug you this same way? Please forgive me for complaining. Help me to turn my murmurings into praises, my complaints into applause. Thank you for taking care of me.

AMEN *and* GOOD NIGHT, GOD

CRISES

God,

Thank you for your peace that goes far beyond my understanding. Today your calming peace buffered me against another one of life's attacks and neutralized my crisis. I pray I will never fail to depend on your promise of strength and support. Your comfort is available to me always—whether in the little, everyday crisis, or a life-threatening one that comes in the dark of night. I don't know what I'd do without your care for me.

CRISES

God,

Have I bothered you too often about bad hair days and hangnails? about spilled milk on a just-mopped kitchen floor? And remember the puppy and the new carpet? I know you hear my prayers for relief from these tiny splinters of life. And you do help me. But today it's something a little more important. My doctor found a lump this morning, Lord. I'm trying to remain confident that everything will turn out OK. But what if it doesn't? How can I get through this? I don't want to leave my family. Not yet. Please provide me your mercies during this critical time. Help me not to panic and question, but to begin and end each day with you instead. Thank you for your faithfulness.

A M E N   *and*   G O O D   N I G H T ,   G O D

CRITICISM

God,

What did you think of my lunch hour today? The criticism flew fast and furious, making me most uncomfortable. As always, I tried to apply your beautiful Golden Rule. You and I had few allies today, Lord. I wish everyone could understand that all of us fall far short of perfection. Yet these imperfect people felt qualified to dish out condemning criticism of another. Would they have been as eager to hear some of their criticism aimed at themselves? There's only one perfect, qualified judge and that one is you. I'm grateful that your judgment of me always will be tempered by your enduring mercy.

AMEN *and* GOOD NIGHT, GOD

CRITICISM

God,

It was hard this morning to take criticism from my boss when I knew I didn't deserve it. It's bad enough for someone to point out my mistakes when I know I'm wrong. But when I've tried my best, I have a difficult time listening to negative evaluation. Help me to remember how it feels to be unjustly criticized so maybe I'll withhold easy disapproval of someone else. Thank you for giving me patience to deal with those who would so quickly find fault with me.

A M E N *an∂* G O O D   N I G H T ,   G O D

CRITICISM

God,

I was a self-appointed judge this morning. All I lacked was a black robe and gavel. I unreasonably attacked his methods. I would have repaired the leaky faucet differently, of course. Quicker, too. But he was the one working on it, and I should have left him alone to do his job. Thank you for his willingness and his good intentions. Please forgive me, Lord, for interfering. Next time help me to hold back my suggestions until they're asked for.

AMEN *and* GOOD NIGHT, GOD

CYNICISM

God,

Living in this world is turning me into a cynic. I fail in my search for integrity and sincerity. All motives seem to boil down to self-promotion. This morning while I pondered these thoughts, my child looked up at me through trusting eyes. Then I realized where innocence can still be found. It dwells in our children, this purity that seeks unconditional love. Thank you, Lord, for showing that same kind of love for me as one of your children. Please refine my thoughts so I'll not automatically think the worst of people as I've been so prone to do lately. Help me to win this struggle, making me worthy of the eternal inheritance you've promised.

A M E N *and* G O O D   N I G H T ,   G O D

DESPAIR

God,

I'm sitting in a puddle of my own tears. I felt desperate all afternoon, so inadequate. What did I do to deserve this, God? Impossible responsibilities added to my already-too-heavy burdens until I wanted to throw up my hands and quit! But you've given me endurance and encouragement before—and you'll do so again and again. Please help me not to give in to despair and give up. Thank you for helping me climb out of this seductive pit of depression. You are my God of Hope.

DESPAIR

God,

I'd just about resigned myself to permanent despair. But now that feeling is like a distant roll of thunder after a rain shower. I'm refreshed, encouraged. I'm so thankful you've answered my many prayers about his critical attitude. I'd given up, Lord—decided it wasn't worth the effort to try to mend things another time. But your love and understanding rescued me from the tidal wave of hopelessness. Please help me always to have hope in your faithfulness.

AMEN *and* GOOD NIGHT, GOD

DESPAIR

God,

I gave in to despondency this morning, convinced that any further effort was useless. I didn't even leave the house all day. I've let the entire day go by without being of use to anybody. I've been totally inefficient, producing absolutely nothing this day. In such a hopeless state of mind, I can't adapt to your purposes. I need your encouragement, Lord, to meet tomorrow with the proper attitude to serve you. Thank you for watching over me when I'm so unpleasant.

AMEN *and* GOOD NIGHT, GOD

DISCOURAGEMENT

God,

Everything I tried to do today just blew up in my face. Nothing turned out right. I felt like I was drowning and no one tried to save me. First, I couldn't take away the awful heartbreak when my child didn't make the team. Then, when my friend heard that his loved one had died, I stood by with nothing but silent sympathy. And when my feelings were walked on, I just kept quiet and hurt some more. Please forgive me, God, for turning to you so late in my frustrations. If my trust in you had been stronger at the beginning of the day, I'd have been more secure all day long. Thank you for always being close by in my bad times. You always throw me a lifeline — I just need to reach for it.

AMEN *and* GOOD NIGHT, GOD

DISCOURAGEMENT

God,

Today all the tiny irritations ballooned into high jumps I couldn't get over. It seems someone always raised the crossbar when I was about to jump. I can only win when I don't try to be my own coach. If I follow your perfect game plan for my life, I won't step out of bounds. Your encouraging cheers will echo in my ears. Thank you for guidance through each day's tough race.

DISCOURAGEMENT

God,

Please, I need an extended leave of absence from life. Let me go away and return when things get better. I just need to get away from it all! I was so irritable today people could hardly stand to be near me. I've allowed my miseries to handcuff me, holding back the person I should be. But wanting to walk away from my discontent won't remove it. Please give me a makeover, Lord, renewing my attitude to conform to your will. Thank you for your encouragement when things close in on me.

ENVY

God,

This morning I wore my envy like a woolen, winter coat. As I noticed how the neighbors get new things, how they prosper, I tightened the coat's belt of resentment around my waist. God, I'd rather have a capacity to love than a capacity to envy. And love and envy can't reside together. There's not room in my heart to embrace them both. Please free me from my envious desires, reminding me that what my neighbors have and do aren't in your plans for me right now. Thank you for showing me one more time that your way is the best way.

AMEN *and* GOOD NIGHT, GOD

ENVY

God,

I tried. I hope I pleased you. My best friend drove over this evening to take me for a ride in her family's new car. It's a Cadillac, Lord! You know how long I've wanted a Cadillac. I told you I'd be happy with our old car until you said it was time for another one. But, God, my best friend! I swallowed a big gulp of pride tonight. I was tempted to be bitter and say to you, "When's *my* turn?!" I really am pleased for my friend, but it was difficult showing it. Thank you for keeping my tongue from saying anything unkind. Forgive me for my envy.

AMEN *and* GOOD NIGHT, GOD

ENVY

God,

All I ask for is your help to handle today's feelings. I saw something I wanted, but I couldn't get it. Then I battled within myself: "You don't need it. . . . But I want it! . . . Forget it. . . . I can't forget it, I've got to have it. . . ." I'm displaying immaturity of mind and spirit, hindering my growth to be more like you, Lord. Thank you for strength to escape from this threatening monster called envy.

AMEN *and* GOOD NIGHT, GOD

ETERNITY

God,

I'm travel weary tonight. Each year the distance to our family reunion seems to be a little longer and takes more out of me. But, oh, what a good time I had getting together with the relatives. Some I only see this one time all year. Thank you for bringing us together again one more time. As much as I enjoyed today, it can't compare with the glorious eternal reunion you're preparing for your family of believers. Thank you for your invitation to me to be a part of this heavenly get-together. I praise you for your grace and mercy through your Son, Jesus, which makes possible your forever family reunion.

A M E N *and* G O O D N I G H T , G O D

ETERNITY

God,

I'm so glad that days like today won't continue indefinitely. I'm ready to swap this life for eternity with you and your unlimited comforts and joys. Thank you for promising that when my stressful residence here on earth ceases, I'll content myself by glorifying you in your kingdom. Then I'll have abiding fellowship with you, Lord, unaffected by time.

FEAR

God,

The thunderstorms rattled windowpanes today. She clung to my hand, her eyes begging me not to leave. I hope my calmness displayed my faith in your promise to shield me when I face frightful situations. When I fear, I'm really doubting your ability to care for me. Thank you, Lord, for taking away my fears when I trust your power and love.

FEAR

God,

I don't fear death. I really don't. But I sure don't look forward to separation from my family and friends when I die. Lord, as much as I long to see you, I can't stand thoughts of not having my loved ones near. If we could all just leave together, like when we go on family vacations! I know your master plan is best, and who am I to question it? So, no, I don't fear death. But attending today's funeral, I felt a growing dread about separation from those I love. When I'm nearing my last breath, God, please take my hand in yours. Help me not to look back toward what I'm leaving but to concentrate on the joys awaiting me with you. Thank you for giving me family and friends to love.

AMEN *and* GOOD NIGHT, GOD

FEAR

God,

My silence screams volumes. How ineffective is my testimony to your protection when I'm confronted by bad weather! I just can't help it, Lord. Today's uncertain skies intimidated me. As the first black clouds rolled across the sun, I rushed home to supposed safety. Please strengthen my faith that you will protect me from harm wherever I am. Increase my boldness in proportion to my great trust in you. Thank you for decreasing my fears tomorrow.

AMEN *and* GOOD NIGHT, GOD

FOLLOWING

God,

It's difficult to start talking with you tonight—like when one of my friends and I lose contact. It's always a little awkward to renew the friendship. I haven't kept good contact with you for a while. I've been so busy and so tired; I just haven't made time for you. I haven't been much use to you lately, or to myself. But I feel a need to reconnect. In my state of wilting uselessness, you can refresh me like you did the woman at the well. Like you refresh the drooping flowers with gentle rain. Please allow me to reestablish our friendship, so instead of being useless in your service, I can be about your business. Thank you for patiently waiting for my return.

A M E N *a n d* G O O D   N I G H T ,   G O D

FOLLOWING

God,

Today I went on ahead of you. And, oh, the going got rough! In my failure, I admitted I should have followed your lead. You're willing to cut through life's jungle for me—but I didn't let you. When I try to do things on my own, I'm not victorious. But when I allow you to lead, your strength covers my vain efforts. I need to start each morning by lining up behind you and moving in the ways you lead. Thank you for reminding me not to get ahead of you.

A M E N *a n d* G O O D N I G H T , G O D

FOLLOWING

God,

I started out today guided only by my own road map. But it didn't label the side roads of bad choices. Or the roads closed by my selfish desires. Not even the numerous bumpy road conditions showed up on my map. But you knew about all those barriers the day held for me. If I'd only checked out my travel plans with you, Lord, you would have led me through my day. And, oh, how much smoother it would have been! Thank you that you care enough about me to have mapped out my life's journey long ago. Please give me stronger faith to trust and follow you every day.

AMEN *and* GOOD NIGHT, GOD

GRANDPARENTING

God,

The slice of humble pie I ate today went down better than I'd expected. You know how I've always been about boisterous babies disturbing me when I eat out. I always felt they infringed on my rights. "Why don't those people keep their babies at home?" I'd criticize. Well! I pray I'll never again be critical of someone unless I've first walked a little way in their shoes. Today I went out to eat for the first time with my new grandchild. Today I was the one with the disturbing baby. I'm so glad other diners didn't stare like I'd done before. Please forgive me for my past behavior toward other little ones. Grandchildren must be for bringing me back down to earth. Thank you for grandchildren.

AMEN *and* GOOD NIGHT, GOD

GRANDPARENTING

God,

It's not like it used to be. We don't live like the Waltons—two or three generations under the same roof, everybody taking care of each other's needs. No, I can't be there with my grandchildren every day. I can't hover over them, trying to protect them from harm. I ached to hold them today, but thank you for letting me hear their sweet little voices over the telephone. Lord, I'll trust you to guard these precious grandchildren, keeping them safe from danger. Please let me be as much a part of their life as possible.

AMEN *and* GOOD NIGHT, GOD

GRANDPARENTING

God,

It's me again. I didn't check myself in time this morning. I too quickly told my daughter what she was doing wrong with her baby. I don't want to offend these new parents with my uninvited opinions. The baby belongs to them. I must let them do the raising. Thank you for letting me be a parent and now a grandparent. I realize that my role in this baby's life, although important, is secondary to that of his parents. Lord, give me enough compassion and patience to be ready when I'm asked to help, but to avoid intruding on this new family unit.

AMEN *and* GOOD NIGHT, GOD

GRIEF

God,

I have to bury my best friend tomorrow. There'll be no more long telephone calls on Sunday afternoons. No more newsy ten-page letters written in interrupted snatches. No more reminiscing about all the happy times we've shared. My best friend won't smile with me again. I stand in the chilled shadow of death. But you, Lord, are the eternal Light that shines from the other side of death's valley. Please light my way through this darkness. Give me courage tomorrow when I say my last good-bye to my best friend. Thank you for taking my place with her.

AMEN *and* GOOD NIGHT, GOD

GRIEF

God,

They all meant well. And I did appreciate their attempts to include me this evening. But nothing on earth can penetrate this desolation. My grief today was equaled only by my continuing loneliness. When will I ever feel whole again? When death wrenched us apart, I tumbled into a blackness that separated me from reality. How do you expect me to endure this, Lord? Help me to know night from day. Help me to reach back and touch something familiar. Thank you for wrapping your love around me for however long it takes me to return to normal. Normal! I'm one of a matched pair now; will normal ever visit me again? May tomorrow's loneliness be less than today's.

AMEN *and* GOOD NIGHT, GOD

GRIEF

God,

Tonight, please replace my sadness with joy. Exchange my misery for gladness. Turn my misfortunes into satisfaction and my trials into victory. Thank you, God, for your supporting hope as I faced all of today's griefs. I release them now into your inviting arms.

AMEN *and* GOOD NIGHT, GOD

GUILT

God,

The excess baggage weighed heavily on my tired shoulders all day. I recognize it for what it is: I feel guilty, and it's eating me up inside. This morning as we all rushed to get out of the house on time, my small child became my second shadow. In my haste, I literally stepped on that second shadow when I turned around. Without mature thought, in hurried frustration, I scolded him for being in my way. I should have hugged instead of scolded! I did hug, but not until tonight when I tucked him into bed. My child hugged me back and said, "I love you," seeming to have forgotten my ugly reaction this morning. Please forgive me, God, for lashing out at my child. Then help me to forget and release this forgiven sin as my child has. Just as you forget forgiven sin. Teach me how to be as kind toward myself as you are toward me. Thank you for your forgiveness.

AMEN *and* GOOD NIGHT, GOD

GUILT

God,

I've carried this bulky load of guilt for a very long time. I realize now that when I spouted off in frustration, I undoubtedly hurt some feelings. Distance prevents me from personally asking for forgiveness. In fact, I don't even know where those people live today. So, what am I to do? Lord, please forgive me for my abusive words spoken so long ago. I sincerely surrender this guilt to you. Thank you for your release.

GUILT

God,

If I had only known more about my options. . . . I thought I had to vote either innocent or guilty. And the other eleven voted alike, leaving me casting the only "guilty" vote. But, Lord, he not only broke our civil laws, he broke your moral laws as well. How could those other eleven ever consider him innocent? They badgered me with pleas of sympathy for his wheelchair-bound mother who needed him out of jail. With pleas for not interrupting his career. All about rights and privileges of the criminal—not a thought about those of the victims. Our final vote was unanimous, and now the young man walks our streets, free to break the same laws again. If only I'd known about my third option: I could have stood my ground and caused a hung jury, reaching no verdict. My guilt over this brings me many nightmares. But I did the best I knew at the time. Thank you, Lord, for whatever comfort you can give my tortured mind.

AMEN and GOOD NIGHT, GOD

IMPATIENCE

God,

First, I couldn't find my car keys. When I did, the phone rang as I was going out the door. Then, as I rushed for the car to start on my long list of errands, you stopped me in my tracks. Even though I was in a hurry, my feet could run no farther when the concert from the trees began. I couldn't see any birds, but their melodies blended into an almost verbal "Have a good day!" I looked up toward the full branches, applauding with my broadest smile. If my neighbors were watching, they must have wondered what I ate for breakfast! I praise you, Lord, for slowing me down. Every piece of your creation is wonderful, not to be taken for granted. Thank you for writing in some patience on my to-do list for today.

AMEN *and* GOOD NIGHT, GOD

IMPATIENCE

God,

Today I questioned your silent answer to my prayers. I fussed at you when you seemingly refused to intervene in my problems. I just couldn't understand it when you didn't change my life for the better as soon as I thought you should. But the timing of events is not mine to determine. Thank you, God, for not turning away from me and my demands. Please teach me how to be as patient with you as you are with me.

AMEN and GOOD NIGHT, GOD

IMPATIENCE

God,

Please stop me when my voice takes on a scolding tone, as it did this morning, when he couldn't remember the bank's phone number even though he calls it at least once a week; or when he can't recall where he put his favorite Saturday shirt; or when he doesn't fold the clean linens just as I would. Please help me not to treat him as another one of our children. I so easily lose patience after helping him with the same matter over and over. Why can't he remember? I do. Please squelch my temptation to gloat in false superiority because he needs my assistance. Or to forget the many times I depend on him in situations where I'm the helpless one. Thank you, Lord, that with consideration we can be a team, each of us filling gaps left by the other. Keep reminding me that love thrives where patience dwells.

AMEN *and* GOOD NIGHT, GOD

INDECISION

God,

Thank you for coming to my rescue today. Satan planted his seeds of doubt in my mind and watered them with his lies. Then, in my indecision, he tossed me about like ocean waves. But ultimately he lost the battle when your strength directed my feet to more solid ground than Satan's consuming quicksand. Help me always to honor my commitment to you, not weakened by compromise and defeat.

A M E N *and* G O O D   N I G H T ,   G O D

INDECISION

God,

I'm like a child in a candy store who's trying to choose between a red lollipop and a yellow one. I've struggled with this all day long, and I'm no closer to a resolution now than when I got up this morning. The whole thing's destroyed my nerves! I've got to get this settled and off my mind, Lord. Why can't I just make my decision and go on? Even if I make the wrong decision, I'll know I didn't act without thinking. Help me learn to make up my mind with more ease, turning all mistakes into lessons. Thank you for leading me in the right direction when I'm confused over my choices.

AMEN *and* GOOD NIGHT, GOD

LONELINESS

God,

I almost drowned in my loneliness today. I felt isolated, without companionship. All around me, others stayed so busy all day, doing their own special things. They all had somebody to share with. But no one wanted to spend their day with me. Your Word promises you won't leave me alone. I claimed that promise today, and you helped me battle my loneliness. Thank you for knowing and caring how I feel.

AMEN *and* GOOD NIGHT, GOD

LONELINESS

God,

Today, loneliness came uninvited and overstayed its welcome. In my isolation, a group offered me their acceptance, and I eagerly grabbed it. What a mistake! I discovered I could still be lonely even in a crowd. Please help me to remember that I don't have to depend on the exaggerated beauty of worldly pleasures and acceptance. Thank you, God, that only your support gives me lasting comfort. So tomorrow, when the world disappoints and the crowds disappear, I'll turn first to you for fellowship.

AMEN *and* GOOD NIGHT, GOD

LOVE

God,

Thank you for teaching me about your brand of love. Today I deflated several problems by loving people the way you do. If only I could remember to do this every day! Your love is unconditional. It doesn't boast or remember wrongs done to it. Your kind of love is not rude or self-centered. It's kind, always protecting. Your love never fails. Please remind me every day to practice your way of loving with everyone in my life.

AMEN *and* GOOD NIGHT, GOD

LOVE

God,

I was so disappointed that I just didn't know if I could trust either of them again. And without trust, could love exist? Seeing my husband at the mall with my friend ignited my suspicions. I was still nursing my doubts this evening when he took me out to dinner for our anniversary. Then I learned that she had been helping him select my anniversary gift when I'd seen them together earlier. Was I ever embarrassed! And somewhat ashamed that I had so easily doubted his commitment to me. Help me always to look for valid explanations before I draw conclusions. Thank you, Lord, that our love will endure this silly misunderstanding.

AMEN *and* GOOD NIGHT, GOD

LOVE

God,

Please help me to respond to love. I find it easier to give love than to receive it. This morning I felt so uncomfortable when they surprised me with a birthday party. Their singing and gifts and wishes for me were too generous. While I almost feel undeserving of it, I do need to receive love. So I'll depend on you to make me more like you so that I can soak up love from those around me. Thank you for loving me.

AMEN *and* GOOD NIGHT, GOD

MATERIALISM

God,

It was such a trivial thing, but I blew it all out of proportion this morning. Everything escalated until I pitched one of my screaming fits. All because I wanted to buy a new pair of shoes but knew I couldn't afford them. Having to deny myself was worse than the unfulfilled desire. I get so weary of scrimping, Lord—cutting corners so the money will last until the next paycheck! You've taught me about this, I know. Please forgive me for misplacing my concerns. Thank you for being patient with me.

AMEN *and* GOOD NIGHT, GOD

MATERIALISM

God,

I'd been waiting for it to go on sale, and today it finally did. I counted my money and checked the bank balance, but I couldn't convince myself to make the purchase. Something kept holding me back. Finally I obeyed hesitation's tug. Thank you, God, for persuading me to walk away from this unneeded desire, this luxury that would only complicate my life.

AMEN *and* GOOD NIGHT, GOD

MATERIALISM

God,

Satan turned my head away from you today. He used this world's beautiful inventions to lure me. I so easily fell into the I-want-one trap. Today in the stereo shop the sounds lulled me into fantasy, and I wanted to bring it all home with me. Please guide me back onto your more eternal path. Help me to realize that, although nice, these temptations offer only temporary enjoyment. Thank you, Lord, that you have promised me unequaled pleasures if I'll remain faithful in your love.

AMEN *and* GOOD NIGHT, GOD

MONEY

God,

I'd heard about it. But I'd dismissed it, refusing to believe it would ever affect me. Before I married, many of my friends told me more of their marital strife happened over money disputes than anything else. That seemed impossible! Now I know it's true. I'm so tired, Lord, so discouraged. No money ever remains after we barely pay the bills. None! It seems whatever the bills total, that's how much money we have. No more, no less. I force myself to stop and be thankful that all the bills do get paid. I try so hard to have just a little bit extra for emergencies, but I can't make it happen. Some weeks are so tight I'm tempted to skip giving my tithe. Really tempted. But so far I haven't done it. That's your part, and it gets paid first. Thank you for blessing my faithfulness by giving me enough money to cover expenses. Please give me strength to continue using my money wisely.

AMEN and GOOD NIGHT, GOD

MONEY

God,

I finally did it! Today I mailed off the last payment. My credit card balance is a beautiful zero. And with your help, God, I intend to keep it right there. Thank you for your support over these past months while I triumphed in paying down instead of charging up on the account. Now I can put it away and have it for emergency use only. I was irresponsible in my spending and careless to create tremendous debt. But now I feel refreshed, released from the cumbersome burden of debt I so foolishly put upon myself. My only debt now is one of gratitude toward you for loving me.

A M E N *a n d* G O O D N I G H T , G O D

MONEY

God,

When I paid the bills this morning, it took almost every penny in the checking account. Will it never end? Nothing on the Visa bill was for me. Nothing! Every purchase had been for the kids. They needed everything I bought, but their needs never stay filled. Every month's end is like a long drought between rains. I realize my children won't live here forever, and the situation will change one day. But right now, the responsibility is overwhelming, compounded by my selfish desire to have a little extra to spend on myself. Thank you for providing funds sufficient to meet the needs. With your help I'll try to be content, believing you'll supply any true need I have.

AMEN *and* GOOD NIGHT, GOD

MONEY

God,

Everybody around me today checked on their savings, keeping track of their investments. They followed every little dip and rise in interest rates and watched the stock market's ups and downs. It seems that monetary gains and losses influence their lives more than dividends you can give them. Please help me never to neglect the safeguarding of my investments with you. Thank you for allowing me a share of your heavenly stock market.

NEED

God,

I don't know if I can talk to you tonight. I may not have anything left for you. I feel all used up. I just give and give and give, and nobody gives to me. They're all lined up with their cups—family, friends, neighbors, coworkers. They act like I'm an artesian well. But I'm not, Lord! I don't have any more to give. I need a transfusion. Please replenish me with your love so I can then love others. With your love coursing through my veins, I can focus on others in need. Please forgive my selfishness. Help me with my priorities—you first and then others and me. Thank you for understanding when I grumble.

AMEN *and* GOOD NIGHT, GOD

NEED

God,

I tried and tried, but still I failed. When I finally realized I'd come to the end of my own resources, then I turned to you. And, of course, you were there, waiting patiently. You had the strength I needed. You waited until I came to the end of myself and stood ready to receive your help. Thank you for always offering all the help I'll accept. Thank you for cushioning my heart's needs with your presence.

AMEN *and* GOOD NIGHT, GOD

NEED

God,

A closed door means nothing to them. Unless, of course, they do the closing. Maybe I should go ahead and install a revolving door to my bedroom so it would be easier for them to get to me. All I wanted was a little privacy in my bedroom to collect my thoughts, to unwind from the stress. I really don't have a room of my own like the children do, you know; my bedroom isn't even mine alone. Sometimes I can snatch a few minutes in the bathroom, but even that's not always guaranteed. Is it selfish of me to want just a little privacy? This afternoon I'd no sooner calmed the argument between the two younger ones when I had to help find clean socks for another. This goes on all day, every day. Will I ever find peace and quiet? Thank you that I can fill the needs of those dependent on me. But please, Lord, remember my needs.

AMEN *and* GOOD NIGHT, GOD

NEED

God,

You're amazing! How do you do it? You always seem to know when I'm at my lowest, when my needs are the greatest. Today you picked me up once again. You convinced me that I didn't have to fail, that you'd support me. You've never disappointed me. Thank you for always meeting me in my precise moment of need.

NEIGHBORS

God,

The new people moved in next door today, making repeated trips from truck to house in the afternoon heat. When I took ice-cold lemonade over to them, you'd have thought I gave them an ounce of gold! They're a young couple from out of town and don't know anybody here yet. They really seemed to appreciate my offer of friendship. I even invited them over later to eat. I think I'll like having them live next door. Thank you for giving me enough courage, despite my shyness, to step out and practice your love to others.

AMEN *and* GOOD NIGHT, GOD

NEIGHBORS

God,

Some of the people living around me don't know you. Some of them don't want to know you. But I keep telling them about you in many different ways. Ways I think you might have approached them. I don't try to hit anybody over the head with a sermon every time we talk. I don't even always do all the talking. Many times I think I can be a testimony for you by what I do just as well as by things I might say. God, please help me to carefully weigh everything I do or say so I won't offend anyone. Thank you for my neighbors.

AMEN and GOOD NIGHT, GOD

God,

If only I possessed a fraction of your patience and loving-kindness! But this morning, as usual, the first thing I did when trouble came was to lash out, pointing the finger of blame. When he said he didn't have his homework finished, I blamed him. But last night, I didn't give him my undivided attention. I didn't even talk to him about his day or offer any help on his homework. I should have encouraged him with his difficult lessons, given him some time. But I didn't, and he went off unprepared. Some of the fault rests with me. Tonight, Lord, help me to examine my motivations and see how far from you I've really drifted. When I'm so quick to grumble and blame, help me to praise you instead. Thank you for giving me some of your qualities to help me with my family.

AMEN *and* GOOD NIGHT, GOD

PARENTING

God,

Today my child looked me in the eye and, in no uncertain terms, said, "I don't like you at all!" Some days their behavior makes me really not like my children, either. But, God, I don't tell them so. My children don't have to like me all the time. But this one child dared to speak those awful, hateful words out loud to me. No hint of an apology crossed the angry little face. Still, I forgive this child for such an emotional outburst. And tonight, as every night, I pray for all my children—that one included. Please protect them from the penetrating hurt of careless words. Thank you for each of my children.

AMEN *and* GOOD NIGHT, GOD

PARENTING

God,

I know I embarrassed him this morning. But I hugged him anyway. Big boys still need love, even though they don't want the whole world to know it. Maybe I should have done the hugging at home before we went to board the bus. Maybe I'll remember next time. It's just that the week ahead with him away at camp is a long time not to have him around. The house will seem empty tomorrow without him and his unique clamor and clatter. I can't stand to think that in a few years he'll probably leave for good. I only want to enjoy the time you've given me with him now. Thank you for opportunities to show him I love him.

AMEN *and* GOOD NIGHT, GOD

PARENTING

God,

I said I'd never do it. But I am. I go off to a job every morning, leaving my little ones in the care of a sitter. I'm away from them most of their waking hours. God, I'm missing so much of their developing years. I didn't see any of them take their first step. I missed their first words. And sometimes in the evenings they call me by their sitter's name! Will they ever understand that I had no choice? That I had to work so we could pay all the bills? Will they feel I abandoned them? Will they forgive me? Thank you for my job. I'm so fortunate it's a good one with a wonderful boss. Please, Lord, help me to find peace of mind tonight over this situation that I can't change.

AMEN and GOOD NIGHT, GOD

God,

It's going to take me quite a while to make amends with my child for this mistake! I questioned him last night when I heard his reason for coming home late. And when I told him it looked like he could have come up with a better excuse than that, he didn't have another word to say in his defense. But this morning when I talked with some of the other parents, I learned there *really was* a flat tire. I know he wanted to say I told you so when I apologized. He only said, "That's OK." Will I ever be able to rebuild his trust in me? Will he ever again depend on me to believe him? Thank you, Lord, that my child has always been truthful, never causing me to suspect him. Please help me to rebuild a mutual trust that will span this strange gulf between us.

AMEN *and* GOOD NIGHT, GOD

PERSEVERANCE

God,

Please give me more perseverance. I gave up too easily today. Discouragement washed over me, and I couldn't keep on any longer. When opposition blocked my progress, I needed to be more persistent. Lord, I needed your protective assurances. Please bless me with a confident attitude when foes seem to outnumber me. I want to remain steadfast, no matter what the obstacles. Thank you for giving me your encouraging strength to stand for and live by your values.

AMEN *and* GOOD NIGHT, GOD

PRAISE

God,

You outdid yourself today! Thank you for the much needed rain you blessed us with. That was enough bounty for one day. But, then, after the rain, you stamped your rainbow across the clearing sky. Only you could form those ribbons of brilliant hues and stretch them across the sky in perfect harmony. Only you would bless my day with such beauty. I praise you for giving me ample portions of your grace and mercy. Thank you for a beautiful day!

AMEN *and* GOOD NIGHT, GOD

PRAISE

God,

You deserve all my praise for putting up with me! I'm worse than my most selfish child ever dared to be. And you continue to shower me with unmerited blessings and support. This morning when I ranted and raved for no good reason, you were still beside me when I quieted down. When I clutched self-pity's cape around me, you patiently urged me out of my cocoon to get involved in my neighbor's needs. Please forgive me when I don't express my gratitude often enough, or when I don't acknowledge that everything I do, I do through your strength and encouragement. May I always thank you for your constant care and love.

AMEN *and* GOOD NIGHT, GOD

PRAYER

God,

Am I doing it right? Are my prayers OK? I just say what I feel. That's the only way I know to talk to you, God. My simple prayers may not make sense sometimes, but at least you know I'm honest. I don't believe you'd listen to me very long if I weren't. And you do listen because you always answer my prayers. Sometimes your answer is, "Not now." But that's an answer, so I know you hear me when I pray. I hope I don't bother you because I pray to you about even the smallest things—like finding a close parking spot when it's raining. But I guess since I pray so much about little things, it's easy for me to quickly pray to you when the really big problems come. Thank you for listening tonight and understanding when I think no one else does.

AMEN *and* GOOD NIGHT, GOD

God,

Without conversation with you, I'd never get through many of my days. Days when naked conflict pushes aside needed compromise. Days when the children fail to meet my expectations or when I fail to meet theirs. And days like today when I'm discouraged to the bone, completely worn out and without hope. Only through talking with you, Lord, can I gain necessary energy to survive each day. Thank you for hearing my petition and thanksgiving as I visit with you tonight.

AMEN *and* GOOD NIGHT, GOD

PRIDE

God,

I depended too much today on the praise of people. Their applause is now only a faint memory. The next time we all get together, their attention probably will rest on someone else. They won't even remember today when I thought I was on top of the world. But the top of this world is a crowded place, Lord, where the stay is often short and the departure sometimes swift. Please forgive me for misplacing my trust in such temporary pleasures, and guide my life in the direction you would have me go. Thank you for helping me keep my confidence in you and your permanent love.

AMEN *and* GOOD NIGHT, GOD

PROMISES

God,

This morning when I promised her a trip to the mall, I didn't think she would even remember. I was only trying to appease her, and I gave my word so lightly. When she came to me at the hour we'd set and found me not dressed for our outing, I could see disappointment replace the excitement on her face and distrust creep into her eyes. Oh, Lord, please forgive me for what I have done. I've twisted what an obligation really means. Please help me to somehow make this up to her and teach her better about true commitment. Thank you for rebuilding her confidence in me.

AMEN *and* GOOD NIGHT, GOD

QUESTIONING GOD

God,

Today was another "Why me?" day. I just don't understand. I really try to obey you, God. Am I not pleasing you? I'm always taking more steps backward than forward. I never feel I'm making any headway but, rather, losing ground in everything I attempt. Can you hear me when I silently scream *why?* Thank you for promising that I'll never have to bear a burden heavier than I can carry. Please continue to encourage me daily. Then I can depend on you and not on my own understanding to see me through such troublesome days.

QUESTIONING GOD

God,

Why must my heart break? Why do people disappoint me? Why do I disappoint myself? Why can't I be happy all the time? Why is there not enough money? Please forgive me for my harshness, but today I needed more than the limited understanding you've given me. It would be much easier to face my trials if I knew some of the reasons why. Please, God, increase my trust in you so I won't demand answers. Thank you for helping me if I will just have enough faith to turn over my days to your care. Even though I may still have questions.

AMEN *and* GOOD NIGHT, GOD

REJECTION

God,

I don't fit into their mold. They laughed at me this morning, stripping away another layer of my self-confidence. Who are they to tell me I don't measure up? As long as I know within myself that I meet the only standards that matter—yours—I don't have to feel rejected. They can only affect my heart if I let them, and I refuse to do so. Thank you for guarding my feelings when I'm rejected for trying to be like you.

AMEN *and* GOOD NIGHT, GOD

RENEWAL

God,

Tonight as I recall today's missed opportunities, I pray for another tomorrow. Tomorrow, when once again you will give me a blank page to fill. Thank you, Lord, for replacing today's tired and faded moments with a new tomorrow. A new tomorrow when you will rejuvenate me, restoring my vigor and excitement. In your kindness, please renew my efforts by cleansing, repairing, and rebuilding my character to fit within your will. Cleanse my thoughts, words, and deeds, making them acceptable for your use.

AMEN *and* GOOD NIGHT, GOD

RENEWAL

God,

I had absolutely no direction today. Like a grocery cart with wobbly wheels. I felt incapable of performing as you expected. Thank you, Lord, for breaking my chains of futility, releasing me to the life you intended for me. Now, instead of serving no useful purpose and being completely ineffective, I feel qualified for your tasks. Please increase my enthusiasm for you.

A M E N *and* G O O D   N I G H T ,   G O D

RIGHTEOUSNESS

God,

You are loving and forgiving. I'm reassured that because of your grace and my faith in you, you declare me forgiven. Please help me never to get so caught up in working for you that I forget what a precious gift you have given me. My good works please you, but that is not why you saved me. It's because of my faith in you that you have handed down to me a "not guilty" verdict in your court of wrath against sin. Thank you for your gift of right-eousness, a gift impossible for me to earn.

AMEN *and* GOOD NIGHT, GOD

RIGHTEOUSNESS

God,

Satan chipped away at my faith all day today. He sometimes broke through at my points of weakness — my desire, my envy, my greed. But bolstered by my faith in you, God, I resisted Satan and withstood his attacks. Through this faith, you forgave my mistakes, exchanging them for a righteousness before you. Thank you for strengthening my faith each day.

AMEN *and* GOOD NIGHT, GOD

SALVATION

God,

Nothing that happened today can overshadow the gift of salvation in your Son, Jesus Christ. Through your grace, rescue some person tonight from sin's darkness. At this moment may someone ask for and find forgiveness, becoming fit for your kingdom. Thank you for Jesus.

SALVATION

God,

I saw it on the faces of so many when I shopped at the mall today, then at the grocery store. Even last Sunday at church. It's so obvious to me that my country has lost its first love—the faith and trust in you that my country's founders even stamped on its buildings and its money. Through your salvation, please bring us deliverance. Lord, help us all to accept your grace and mercy. Thank you that you can regenerate this nation and give it your positive blessings. I rejoice tonight that you love us enough to save us from destruction if we will turn to you.

A M E N *and* G O O D   N I G H T ,   G O D

SATAN

God,

Did you see him? Of course you did. Satan really showed himself today! He turned up everywhere I went. He lurked around all day long, telling me I wasn't doing a good job. I should have stopped at the first hint of his presence. But I kept on, letting him weaken my self-esteem at every corner. Finally I did call on you, God. Thank you for leading me away from Satan's entrapments. If only I'd called on you earlier, instead of just swatting at him like I would at a pesky fly! When I allow you to help me fight Satan, he can't win. Satan's like the schoolyard bully—he'll run away when the odds shift against him. Tomorrow when he first shows up, I'll call for you. Please continue to help me resist Satan so he'll stay away.

AMEN *and* GOOD NIGHT, GOD

TEMPTATION

God,

When that temptation flew smack into my face, I wavered for just a moment. But I counted the cost of one little bit of enjoyment against your promises of eternal joy. Then I hid behind your strong, gentle love, which enabled me to push back from Satan's table. Help me always to realize you can give me much more than Satan could ever offer! Thank you for your shelter when temptation swirls around me.

AMEN *and* GOOD NIGHT, GOD

TEMPTATION

God,

After I survived temptation this morning, I felt stronger in my faith, more ready to do your will. Whatever way I respond to Satan's decoys, temptation can be a valuable proving ground of my faith in you. Thank you for strengthening me through temptation.

TEMPTATION

God,

I almost fell today. I only needed to take one more step—a step away from responsibility into abandonment. I felt an unfamiliar high when someone still found me attractive after these many years of housework and child rearing. The enticement became so strong it almost overcame my better judgment. Lord, I don't know exactly what happened, but when I came to my senses, I was sitting in the car in my driveway. Thank you for rescuing me; for somehow yanking me back to reality. Back to my home, my family, myself. If I'd yielded to my desires this morning, I'd have become another casualty of the world's promises of pleasure. Please forgive my weakness and strengthen my resolve.

AMEN *and* GOOD NIGHT, GOD

God,

Unspeakable joy is mine tonight as I reflect on my possessions. Oh, I don't have a lot of money or big cars or fine clothes. As satisfying as those things might be, they're not what bring me contentment. My pleasure comes tonight from your promises of peace, comfort, and loving care. These things I hold dear to see me through the certain miseries of life. These gifts from you are permanent. They can't be used up and won't go out of style. Thank you for keeping your promises, never dampening my great delight in you.

AMEN *and* GOOD NIGHT, GOD

THANKSGIVING

God,

I praise you for the miracles of today. I'm thankful for your many blessings. Help me to be positive, not grumbling daily or taking for granted your many good provisions. You can do more for me than I could even imagine! May I never forget to offer you praise and thanksgiving.

AMEN *and* GOOD NIGHT, GOD

THANKSGIVING

God,

Today I failed to appreciate all the beauty surrounding me. Please help me to notice the pleasures in your creation. I don't want to miss the joy of the smallest blossom's aroma, the velvet of the inside of a puppy's ear, the strong cry of the youngest newborn. Or the splash of color in each new rainbow or the welcome glass of water on a hot summer day. May these wonderful miracles always bring me gladness of heart, filling me with immeasurable love for you. Thank you, Lord, for giving me time in your world for a while.

AMEN *and* GOOD NIGHT, GOD

THANKSGIVING

God,

Do you feel like saying, "What is it this time?" whenever I say your name? Please forgive me for complaining and begging all day long today, never taking time to acknowledge the many blessings I already have. It seems I always think of myself, pestering you to meet my demands. If all my prayers the rest of my life were only ones of thanksgiving, they could never thank you enough for what you graciously give me. My family, friends, and community. Material possessions that make life comfortable, if not luxurious. Your love that binds it all together and makes each day worth living.

AMEN *and* GOOD NIGHT, GOD

THANKSGIVING

God,

Your whole creation moves in perfect harmony: the day and night, the land and sea; the young and old. Thank you, Lord, for your perfection everywhere. Please help me always to balance my petitions with equal amounts of gratitude. May thanksgiving always be the theme of my conversations with you.

AMEN *and* GOOD NIGHT, GOD

WAYWARD CHILDREN

God,

Why does it have to be so heartbreaking? It's like pushing a chain to keep this one child in line with the rest of the family. It's becoming a battle I seem to be losing. All these children are mine, and I've tried to raise them the same, but they're not all turning out like I intended. But, they'll always be my children whatever the outcome. Help me to continue my efforts to raise them as you desire and never give up on any child. Thank you for reminding me that you made my children to be individuals.

A M E N *and* G O O D N I G H T , G O D

WAYWARD CHILDREN

God,

She wouldn't listen when I tried to tell her, when I tried to explain the outcome of such an unsound decision. There was no way her reasoning could have brought lasting security. Now she knows. Her life has been difficult, full of anxiety and uncertainty. But nothing can be changed now. It's done, behind us. Still, as bad as it was, the bleakness of her past life makes today's blessings shine all the brighter. Thank you, Lord, for keeping her from complete destruction, for reaching down and protecting her until she turned to you. And thank you for cradling my heart through the years, patching its daily cracks with your compassion. For bringing my child back to me today more lovable than the day she left.

AMEN *and* GOOD NIGHT, GOD

WAYWARD CHILDREN

God,

I pray again for my child. I don't even know where he is tonight. We're in this motel in a strange city because the authorities thought they had found him. We came to identify the body. Today was the hardest day of my life. I dreaded the finality, yet I anticipated the relief from uncertainty. But the young man's body we viewed did not belong to us. Tomorrow we'll go back home to wait some more, hopeful again that the next telephone call will be from him. Asking us to pick him up someplace just like when he was a little boy. I'd gladly forgive him all the anguish he's brought me if only he'd come back. Thank you for watching over him, shielding him from harm. When he does return, Lord, please help us to mend broken hearts and hurt feelings. Lead us toward healing compromises we can all live with. Please just bring him home to me. Please.

A M E N *and* G O O D N I G H T , G O D

WEARINESS

God,

My batteries gave out on me today, and I still had so much left to do. Things I thought no one else could do. I push this human body almost past its limits, don't I? You're the only one who will not get tired. Only you will endure. You promised you would refresh me in my exhaustion if I place my faith in you. Thank you for holding me up when my own strength fades.

AMEN *and* GOOD NIGHT, GOD

WEARINESS

God,

I started out this morning already behind! I didn't even finish yesterday's list. I'm so tired I can't see straight. I used to be able to stay at least one step ahead. Now I can't even keep up. I'm standing knee-deep in discouragement. The only reason I keep trying to catch up is your promise of rest from all this. I plan to depend on you to see me through. You're strong when I'm weak. Thank you for holding me up. Thank you for giving me a better day tomorrow.

AMEN *and* GOOD NIGHT, GOD

WEARINESS

God,

I've said yes too many times until finally today everything caught up with me in a big way. Or was it you, Lord, who caught up with me, applying the brakes to my frantic activities? I felt so silly lying there on the floor with my feet propped up higher than my head. The decorations had to be put up on time, and I guess I thought I was the only one who could do them. But, you know, when I became unable to do any more, those decorations somehow got finished. And they looked good, too. Thank you for showing me I'm not indispensable. Maybe if I let some of these jobs be passed around to others, I'll get more rest, take better care of myself. Then I'll be refreshed for the tasks I must do.

AMEN *and* GOOD NIGHT, GOD

WEARINESS

God,

If I couldn't have turned all my problems over to you today, I probably would have collapsed under their weight. Day after day, week after week, I've labored against the odds. Working outside my home, working when I get home. Getting up early to do laundry before breakfast. Going grocery shopping after putting the children to bed. Searching vainly for a few minutes for myself. I feel like the children's train set—once the train starts, its wheels carry it around and around, no exit anywhere. But today, God, I just stepped off and into your waiting calm. Thank you for renewing my strength to do what I must do. Thank you for helping me carry my heavy load.

A M E N *and* G O O D   N I G H T ,   G O D

WITNESS

God,

Thank you for choosing me long before I chose you. Thank you for allowing me to be a member of your family. I want to please you, God. I pray that I will never disappoint you and that others will always recognize me as yours. I want to live up to the expectations of your family name. Thank you for loving me as your child.

WITNESS

God,

Forgive me for identifying with the world today. It was easier to go along than to be different. Thank you, God, for your strength to help me prevail tomorrow when I don't agree with what the rest of the crowd wants to do. Please renew my efforts to be Christlike.

WORRY

God,

I'm afraid I let concern overstep its boundaries today. It's natural to have healthy concern for my family, for my duties, and for my life. But today I didn't share those concerns with you, Lord. And if I don't let you help me, my concerns shift into worry. Thank you for helping me to have prudent concern, not fruitless worry.

WORRY

God,

You've got the hairs on my head numbered. You know what happens to the tiny sparrows. You clothe the lilies and watch over the ravens. What, then, did I have reason to worry about today? Strengthen my faith in you, God, so that tomorrow and forever I will feel assured of your constant care for me. Thank you for placing value on my life. You know my every need, and your provisions are abundant.

WORRY

God,

Again, I've tried to help you by meddling. I wanted solutions to happen today on my timetable. I was too headstrong to adjust myself to your agenda. But you got my attention. With loving grace, you nudged me back into my place. And then you took care of my concerns the way you'd planned to do all along. You've convinced me, again, that you're greater than my every heartache. Please help me to remember that you're in control, not me. You can make it better. I love you, God.

AMEN *and* GOOD NIGHT, GOD

I will lie down and sleep in peace, for you alone, O Lord, make me dwell in safety. *Psalm 4:8*

To him who is able to keep you from falling and to present you before his glorious presence without fault and with great joy—to the only God our Savior be glory, majesty, power and authority, through Jesus Christ our Lord, before all ages, now and forevermore! Amen. *Jude 1:24-25*

DATE DUE

MAY 0 2 1997			